docs

DOGS

Fiona Pitt-Kethley

SINCLAIR-STEVENSON

First published in Great Britain 1993
by Sinclair-Stevenson
an imprint of Reed Consumer Books Limited
Michelin House, 81 Fulham Road, London SW3 6RB
and Auckland, Melbourne, Singapore and Toronto

Copyright © 1993 by Fiona Pitt-Kethley

ISBN 1 85619 285 7 (paperback)

A CIP catalogue record for this book
is available at the British Library

Typeset by Rowland Phototypesetting Limited
Bury St Edmunds, Suffolk
Printed and bound in Great Britain
by Cox & Wyman Ltd, Reading, Berks

Contents

Acknowledgements

Some of these poems have appeared in the *London Review of Books*, *The International Food and Wine Magazine*, *Gown*, *Bête Noire*, *Poetry Review*, the *Observer*, *Oxford Review*, *Spectrum*, *Pearl*, *Penthouse*, the *Sunday Express* and anthologies – *The State of the Language*, *The Orange Dove of Fiji* and *Grandchildren of Albion*.

The two articles in the notes appeared in shorter forms in the *Independent*.

Birth

Five times the seven-year cycle of my skin's
almost erased the scars I got at birth.
The forceps never even left a mark
on my tough skull. Covered in blood, alone,
I used my untried nails to track my face
and gouged eleven claw marks by the mouth,
before they wrapped my hands like boxing-gloves.

At thirty-nine, my mother'd lain four days
in a slow labour, too relaxed by all
the ante-natal exercise to have
the will to push. I was her only child.
For the last few hours her feet were caught up
in stirrups, while I was dragged out.
I came, screaming protest on a high C.
Babies – one look at their angry faces
tells us they know wrath before words.

For years, my favourite game was getting out
against the odds. My mother'd seal the bed
around me, tuck it, try to hold me in,
while I, by struggling, fought my way to air –
'Here I am all covered with mud,' I'd laugh –
content with fairly easy victories.

But what of those other more complex births?
The in-built pattern of my life decrees
struggle and effort before everything –
seven years to my first book (rejections scar),
more years to free myself from poverty
(uncertain freedom that could well slip back).
And love – five years' emotion on one man –
and I am still as stuck, as on my own.

Next life span, gods, give me a silver spoon
and every honour handed on a plate,
or let my mother drop me in a hedge.
I want an easy birth – no fights, no scars.

Iconoclasts

'Our baby fucked the Bible!' – boastful Dads
Love to reveal the talents of their lads.
With flexing fingers and a rapist's look,
His little monster grabs their only book.
Genesis, Exodus are soon no more . . .
Leviticus and Numbers hit the floor.
Old and New Testaments are next divorced,
Major and minor prophets rolled and forced
Into his porringer of puréed pear.
He's bored to buggery in his high chair.

Babies are all iconoclasts by will,
But mostly lack the strength to do much ill.
Now get a toddler on to wrecking spines
And you'll be deep in debt with library fines.
Kids roger books – just look at Rupert Bear
And splattered, ravaged annuals everywhere.
Girls' and Boys' Owns and well-shagged Andrew Langs,
Too screwed to salvage, give collectors pangs
And prove Victorian brats were just as bad –
'Seen but not heard', they still fucked books like mad.

What masochistic urge makes authors trust
Their earthly fame to the destructive lust
Of pre-school psychos, full of infant rage,
Who leave their mark on every goddam page?
I'd call it intellectual suicide.
A child of any brainpower will decide
On its own reading list from *adult* stuff.
'Bring out the *Kama Sutra*,' Darren cries,
'Janet and John's a pack of bloody lies!'

Arts Council grants vary from year to year –
Poetry, prose – so taxpayers will infer
Their money is judiciously employed.
In '89, the grants were all enjoyed

2

By those who'd written children's books – a strange
Condition limited one prize's range –
The books must be for kids 'aged 0 to 9'.
How would Arts Council policy define . . .
'A nought-year-old's an unborn girl or boy . . .'?
Foetuses kick, some even jump for joy –
St Januarius was the latter breed –
But before birth, even Saints cannot read.

'Doth God exact day labour light denied?'
Must learning start while we are still inside?
Should unborn babes scan comics in the womb,
Using a torch in its ancestral gloom?

What next? A grant for chap-books by a don
For artful sperms to rack their brains upon?

Psychologists

At seven I went to a psychologist.
These days, I sometimes meet them socially.
Some of them say that they have read my work
(they only seem to like the bits on sex)
and let me know what I have always known –
there's nothing wrong with my promiscuous life.

But then, they start to ask about my youth . . .
I know their game. I see that eagerness,
crossed with a species of mock-innocence . . .
till disappointment dawns.

I got on well with both my parents. Shame!
It shouldn't be allowed. They'd hoped I'd longed
to fuck my Dad or murder poor old Mum
or, at the very least, had been abused.

Hugo

We drawing-pinned a notice on the gate
offering half-Siamese black and white kittens.
They were Tess' first litter. We just had
three – Dapple, Hugo and Blownoutus – left.

Dapple was dappled and Blownoutus fat,
but Hugo looked extremely posh, I thought,
a slim black Manx with lovely slanting eyes –
definitely the wicked-squire type.

An evil girl from Acton picked that one.
'Dead common!' my mother said. 'Still, I suppose
she fancies him . . .'

Just seven days later they came round.
'He won't settle!' she said.

He had a tight bright yellow collar on –
its identity disc was stamped 'SQUEAKER'.
With his bag of horsemeat tied round his neck,
he looked – dead common.

The girl had brought some liquorice allsorts
to shut me up. 'I bet she stole them though,'
Mum said. 'She seems the type.' I didn't care.
I had the sweets and I'd got Hugo back.
I took him straight to bed.

Dogs

Young men, like pups, can be somewhat unformed.
Unless you're certain of their pedigree,
it's hard to see how they'll mature and grow.
(Alsatians will fuck dachshunds now and then.)

A man who has some mileage on the clock
in theory would be best. You know the worst –
how much his hair is likely to recede,
his face to fold, as 'character' comes out.
(Furrows look better on the land than skin –
the worst one is a constipated frown –
laughter lines are the most forgivable.)
Auden grew wrinkled as a shar-pei dog.
Most only reach the pug or bloodhound stage.

I've tried 'the older man' – the problem's not
the looks. It's the god-awful temperament.
Rottweiler-grumpiness sets in with age.
I'll stick to pups who're younger than myself –
they've got more stamina for exercise
and better natures, willing to be trained.
I'll whistle and they'll come, fetch, carry, beg.
Of course, I wouldn't take on one *too* young –
I'd certainly prefer him weaned from Mum.

Old dogs, it's said, *cannot* be taught new tricks –
and those they have are all predictable.
They guard their kennels self-importantly,
mark out their territory in wind and piss,
bark righteously for any trifling cause,
follow the pack in every bloody thing.
All their affection's of the boisterous kind –
they're awfully free with dandruff, spittle, hair.
The eviller ones are snappish with young kids,
chase those who're weaker than themselves (like sheep),
seize you and won't let go, roger your legs,

lose socks, worry old bones and bury things.
And *all* take leaks at frequent intervals.

Don't get me wrong – I'm partial to a dog.
I blame their breeders for the way they're trained.

Meanness

I don't mind men who're tight as a duck's arse.
I'm not a grabbing, greedy, gold-digger.
Women who're after presents all the time,
who do sod-all, yet feel they should be kept
are just *dishonest whores*. What they deserve's
old age upon the dole in shabby clothes,
when all the looks that they have used are gone.

Why am I slightly anti generous men?
Their treats and gifts are like the Trojan Horse.
Nothing comes free in life. And I dislike
the way that most assume we can be bought,
perhaps boast to their friends how much they've spent,
talk of the value had for hotel costs,
treat us as assets like their brand new cars.

My ideal man wouldn't have to give me gifts.
I'd buy my round and split a restaurant bill.
(His miserliness should not be *too* complete –
I'd like him to be generous to himself
with things like toilet-paper, shampoo, soap.
I'd rather that he dressed reasonably well –
tastefully casual Oxfam things would do –
it needn't cost enough to break his heart.)
What would *I* want of him? The same I give –
good looks, good conversation and good sex.

There's just one meanness I won't tolerate –
a cautious lack of passion in a man.
Laodiceans should be celibates.
You hear them weighing up the pros and cons.
Can they be bothered to fix up a date –
next week? next month? And is it worth their while?
They'll ring – eventually – but far too late.
They only think about themselves, not how
that long, unflattering hesitance will affect.
Ungiving, closed-in, useless impotents –
too tight to give away a drop of sperm.

Shylock

'I am a Jew. Hath not a Jew eyes? hath not a Jew hands,
organs, dimensions, senses, affections, passions? . . . If you
prick us, do we not bleed? If you tickle us do we not laugh? If
you poison us do we not die?'

I like Shylock. When playing him at eleven
I learned to sympathise and see his point of view.
(My version was more Sweeney Todd than Jew.
I pulled my hair round, tied up as a beard,
wore a loose preaching-gown and velvet cap
and brandished mother's bread knife in the Court.)

He had more guts and more integrity
than all the Gentile bastards in that play.
(The noble Portia I do not admire –
for all her estimable logic in the dock,
all she attained was union with a wimp
who obviously preferred his man-friend's charms,
yet needed marriage to a girl with cash.)

Some words of Shylock's still remain with me,
24 years away from playing his part –
the speech in which he states the outcast's case
and pleads the same humanity for Jews.

The man I loved – a bastard-Gentile-type –
saw me as far less human than Mankind,
less human than the women in his life,
especially his wife (although she screws around
and treats him like a dog). I'm just
'a character', he's said as much – far 'too
eccentric' for his love. (Do *I* not bleed?)

Though not a Jew, I am a Jew to him.
Feelings? I haven't got the things to hurt.

If I had 'Jewish gaberdine' *he*'d spit
on it for sure – well, metaphorically.

And yet this Gentile craves what I have got –
no, unlike Shylock, I've no cash to lend –
he'd like my sympathy for all *she*'s done.
(It doesn't occur the tales might cause me pain.)
And, curiously, he *also* wants my love –
though he's no thought of ever paying back.

Revenge is sweet – almost as sweet as sex.
No smart-arse Portia'll spring to his defence.
'The quality of mercy is not strained . . .'
Mercy? I've not seen much of it around,
'strained' or unstrained. I'll get my pound of flesh.
I've learned my lesson from poor Shylock's case –
I'll settle for the bastard's blood as well.

Rubber Plant

Take the damn thing – I've hardly space to breathe.
It dominates me – fills my living room.
You won't acknowledge it as yours? Well then,
I'll dump it on your doorstep one dark night.

I'm talking of our love. Yes, I say *ours*.
You needed it to prop your ego up,
yet show surprise at how your seed has grown
and blame me for its inconvenient size.
But why? You fed and watered it. Yes, you're
responsible as Doctor Frankenstein!

Long-Stemmed Rose

A fan once sent a long-stemmed rose to me
in its own Guernsey-postmarked cardboard
                                    box,
frost-bitten, tightly furled in cellophane –
unappetising as a condomed cock.
I took it out, nicked off a bit of stem
(as the instructions said) and stuck it in
the slit provided in its plastic pot.
Dead from day one – it never opened out.

David had said he was my Mr Right
in 20 pages (quite illiterate).
He told me by what trains he would arrive
on Christmas Eve and leave on Boxing Day.
(He wanted value for his sodding rose,
promising to be 'horny at 4 a.m.')
He offered me the sun and moon – as men
will do when they have little else to give.

Machine photos that only cost a pound
aren't often a pretty sight – and *his* was worse.
I shall assume he'd sent the best of four –
Madame Tussaud's, I'm sure, could use the rest.

The Book Trade

Mike's seen my photo in a magazine
and thought it only fair to send me his –
headless with almost all the genitals
modestly covered with a clutched white towel.
Fans spend three ninety-nine and think a book
is not enough for that amount of cash –
the poet's body ought to be thrown in.
This week's free offer? Air miles? Green Shield Stamps?

Well, Mike, though I am not about to be
your 'partner on the swinging couples scene',
I'll spare a little time to talk finance.
Of that three ninety-nine I get a tenth
minus my agent's ten per cent plus VAT;
about a third goes to the bookseller;
the rest of it's the publishers'. By rights –
if anybody should be screwed . . .

Independent Means

My home's my base. The voices on the phone
are cash and work. The postman brings me cheques.
I have more faith in those than billets doux.
Money is freedom – it's worth fighting for.

Life's an adventure – roundabouts and swings.
My time's my own. I start and end the day.
No union leaders tell me when to strike.
I have no boss and therefore can't be sacked.
(Poor nine-to-fivers think I'm vulnerable.
Their eggs are in one basket. Mine are not.)

I lead a freelance life in everything.
(The price of that's eternal vigilance.)
I make my own rules, find new ways to win.
(The Law is not an ass – just awfully slow.)
Pitt-Kethley's Law is faster for results.

My method's simple – putting pressure on
Achilles' heels until the heels give in.
A year of nagging got me back the rights
on books a publisher had bought too cheap.
Last month *New Woman* tried to halve the fee
they'd offered for an article. I went –
two letters and no money on – and sat
(new-womanlike) down on their office floor.
The editor was called. I said I'd wait,
hinting I'd food and books to last a week,
until I got my cheque . . .

A muesli bar and half a Trollope on –
four hours – I got the cash. (I thought I would.)

Man is no island, more a microcosm.
In fighting for ourselves, we fight for everyone.

Bird Watching

Bad men, it's said, behave 'like animals'.
(If beasts should ever imitate mankind
we'd never call our lives our own again.)

Next life, I'm going up the social scale.
Four feet? Too risky! Men might have my hide.
A bird? No chicken though – they're factory-farmed.
I'll settle for a gull's life by the sea.

My first few years, a dopey speckled thing
with sloe-black eyes and long St Trinian's legs
like wrinkled stockings with brown leather feet,
I start by picking mussels from the beach
and bathe in boating lakes among my kind.
Then, growing bolder, I will leave my home
to fly from coast to coast, try city life
and feast on junk, join ferries bound for France
or ride the thermals high above the cliffs.

At five, with all my childhood freckles gone,
demure in white and grey, I seek a mate –
bigger and stronger, but much like myself,
with kind, straw-coloured eyes as mild as mine,
an orange beak and long thin, clapper-tongue,
a deep pink throat that opens roaring wide
for bleakly-operatic Cockney cries.

I keep my head down when I see the gull
I want (males like that act). Convinced I'm not
a threat, he lets me move into his pad.

In Spring, I lead him on with cooing cries.
He says sex feels like flying on my back.

He takes his turn upon our clutch of eggs
and feeds me while I'm housebound – that's his job.

We kick the heads of humans who come near.
I test this mate of mine – if he protects
our mutual investment, then I'm his
for life. Divorce looms otherwise . . .

Our marriage, made in heaven, seems to last –
no money problems, mortgage, DIY –
the roof we share never cost *us* a cent.
Our nest's a mess, but we don't care a toss.
We're out a lot, you see. Our kids are fine –
a little stupid, true – but they will learn.
Our sons can fly at least – well, just about.
It's time they left. It's time we were alone.

This incarnation round I feed four gulls.
They breakfast shortly after dawn each day.
The males knock on my window with their beaks.
While I look out at them, the birds look in.

Next time, when I become a herring-gull,
I hope to keep some data in my head . . .
Charm humans and make friends of them.
Councillors order culls, believing gulls
will multiply by two by two by two:
endear yourself to those who'll make a fuss
about the 'sacredness of life' and tell
those nincompoops no creature breeds to form
and there are casualties from storms and oil.
Charm humans, but don't get too close to them . . .
Keep off their runways and their aeroplanes,
don't tread on glass, be careful of their tips,
eschew the plastic from their packs of beer
and never catch their tit-bits in your beak –
just let them drop – then look before you eat.

Living off the Land

Lawns leave me cold; Wordsworth can keep his daffs.
Veg. can be handsome too. I'm not taken in
by roses and geraniums. I'm not
seduced by gaudy clashing flowers.
Give me a row of purple cabbages,
the solid beauty of an artichoke,
the sexy scent of broad bean flowers.

All the best gardens should be eatable –
fruit trees, not flowering shrubs, and useful herbs
(their subtle coloured foliage adds some class).

Visitors look appalled at my small plot –
30 by 40, bounded by brick walls.
(They don't appreciate its fertile charms –
last year the spinach ended seven feet high.)
Conventionally, they like my woodland bed
beneath the useless flowering cherry tree –
all bluebells, primroses and celandines.
(I nicked them from a building site nearby –
a rescue job before the concrete came.)
The rest's more to my taste.

I have two apple trees. The Worcester's fine –
a handsome little heavy-laden tree.
The Golden Delicious though's not up to much.
(The Garden Centre overpersuaded me.
I'd wanted cookers, but, Bramleys, they said,
would need another tree to fertilise.
As if bees couldn't cross a wall or two!)
The tree's a sorry sight and accident prone.
Year one – a boy bore branch and fruit away;
year two – a cast-iron gutter from the tower
sliced it in two; year three – the hurricane.
These days I heap the earth about its heel
in hopes the tree'll revert to its dwarf stock.

The middle patch where these two trees reside
has scattered lettuce, rocket, radishes
(and spinach of course) mixed up with strawberry plants –
200 spread from 3. Where they run out
I grow potatoes from old peelings' eyes.
Then comes the rockery – tomato plants.
My tom cat always rogers tabbies there
beside a lily of the Nile and vine.
(That sodding vine I call my worst mistake,
brought on by fantasies of home-made plonk.
The snails are always first to get the grapes.)

Herbs line the sides. My rosemary's so big
I lagged it to the plum tree with old tights.
I eat the flowers in honey, drink the tea –
I thrive on strange tisanes (and wash in them) –
marjoram, fennel, tansy, lemon balm,
sage – plain and purple, thyme, angelica,
vervain, verbena, borage, wormwood, rue.
Other herbs I grow solely for flavouring –
ramsons (wild garlic), parsley, chervil, chives,
lovage, sweet Cicely, two kinds of mint.

I tolerate all flowers that I can eat –
nasturtiums, violets, forget-me-nots.
Weeds can be tasty too – I recommend
shepherd's cress sandwiches (with wholemeal bread)
and puréed good-King-Henry served with fish.
I like to find a use for everything.

Jealousy

I've never really liked the look of her:
her head is flattish, with no room for brains,
her skin is overcooked – lamb's liver-brown –
her eyes are narrowed like a rattle snake's,
her mouth is wide, but never, never smiles,
her teeth are long like an Etruscan skull's.

What lies beneath? Petite as a dried stick,
on bandy pins that couldn't catch a pig.

Still, if that's what he likes . . .

Trompe-l'oeil

She found a small building
amongst trees,
domed, the windows cracked, the heavy door ajar,
inside, a litter of papers on marble,
a statue in a niche, two wooden benches
and above, a ceiling
painted with trompe-l'oeil
by some late admirer of Mantegna,
a domed sky with three figures
looking down from a balcony –
an old man, a young man and a boy.

Then she sang a few notes
tentatively,
drew herself up –
the bow on an old violin –
and gave birth to a new voice,
asexual, Baroque,
Cavalli-god-like, the voice of a gold-breasted Cupid,
half castrato, half mezzo-soprano,
liquid as ectoplasm.

That autumn morning
as she sang
a scatter of snowflakes
fell from the fresco
and the wind blew chill from the door.
From a small crack in the clouds
the sky-rain dripped slowly,
blue-white with tempera.
And she sang
challenging those who stood above
till a piece of the sky
came and blotted her out
while the three men watched from the parapet
in the drenched and rotten timbers

that lay behind the clouds.
And the door shut fast
with the wind.

Astronomy

Starry nights leave me cold. The sky's all Greek
To me – a spangled mess. I'm up the creek
Without a paddle when it comes to names
Of constellations – boringest of games.
How can a rational human being compare
A clutch of spatters with a bull or bear?
My brain has little storage left for stars –
It's useless info – like the names of cars.
I will forget, let all bar two go hang –
Castor and Pollux make good rhyming slang.

Poem for St Valentine's Day

Man gives and woman takes. She's wined and dined.
She gets red roses and he pays. She lets
Him have his way with her if she is 'kind
As she is fair'. He's paid by what he gets –
Favours for prezzies, kinks for eats and drinks.
It's 'trick or treat' as the old bargain's made.
Equality goes down the drain. She thinks
The more he spends, the finer accolade.
'Thirty for *straight*, or twenty quid for *French*' –
The King's Cross girl is a more honest whore.
Her game's survival, up before the Bench,
Fined more than wined or dined. Yet she's a pearl
Compared with the old-fashioned take-all girl.
Her tariff's fixed; the punters know the score.

Romance is prostitution at its worst –
A pack of sentimental lies immersed
In vile commercialism. The large bouquet
Sent by a lover on St Valentine's day
Is full of open blooms in spite of frost.
(Rich businessmen don't stop to count the cost
Of using toxic chemicals to bring
An early blossoming, unnatural spring
Beneath the polythene. Their workers tell
Of painful symptoms, never feeling well.)
The buds arrive tied neatly, paper-cased,
Morticians' specimens, lying open-faced
Within their cardboard coffins and we give
Them water – for a while they seem to live.
A week or two – they fade, the petals drop,
A stinking vase is all we're left with. Stop,
And think before you make the florists glad.
'Flowers get to her' the Interflora ad
Declares – 'get to' – arrive? Or does it mean
That women everywhere are thought so green
(And cheap) that men can have their way

23

For ten carnations in a floral spray?

I'd much prefer a man to give me seeds –
I'm quite green-fingered with rare herbs and weeds.
Seeds are fit emblems for a long affair,
Growing and ripening with a little care.
And nurturing them is fun. You never *really* know
How many or how large your plants will grow.
OK, I know a photo's on the pack
And info – height etcetera – on the back.
But can the flowers and vegetables read?
My chervil's metamorphosed to a weed,
Triffid-like spinach springs up all around,
Red cabbage cross-breeds, populates the ground,
Purpling all leaves with consanguinity,
Forget-me-nots spread to infinity.

Some men prefer to make gifts edible,
Wanting their women fatly beddable.
Myself, I'm not for boxes of Milk Tray
Delivered by Action Men who rush away
Before the *real* action starts. They drop
From 'copters, swim the Hellespont, don't stop
Till Romeo-like they scale their ladies' walls,
Then – abseil off again. They've got no balls.
Let's hope the girls share their Turkish Delight
Or Raspberry Ripples with some other knight –
One more prepared to stay till morning's light.
Some survey once decreed Brits eat ten pound
Of sweets apiece per year. Another found
Two and a half men's the average woman's quota –
No, not each month – they're her whole lifetime's rota.
My year's one Mars Bar and six mints (approx.) –
It seems I've had their men, they've had my chocs.

I've proved that I'm immune to flowers and sweets.
Candlelight dinners aren't my sort of treats,
Where all's arranged so that the darkness covers
The features of less fanciable lovers.

Sentiment and romance are best for pairs
Where there's grave inequality. His hair's
Quite gone, he's wrinkled, famous, rich;
She's nobody – but a designing bitch.
She's younger than his daughter, but she'll stand
His fumblings – well, it's worth five hundred grand –
A year or two and the divorce comes through.
He'd thought she loved – he's old *and* senile too.
Power is an aphrodisiac we're told.
Bullshit! A grabbing woman goes for gold.

Some lovers long for 'ambience' – soft lights,
Soft music, lingering strolls on starry nights.
I'd rather neon lights than moons in June;
The bed back home's a warmer place to spoon.
At night, the great indoors has more appeal.
I like the snug controlled domestic feel –
A fire you can turn on, a TV too,
A book, a flask of Perrier and You.
(I've nothing against wine, but not all men
Are up to scratch after glass nine or ten.

Before you settle for 'your place or mine?'
Even before you dance or drink or dine –
You must decide upon a meeting place.
That's easy? Don't be sure in every case.
A man I met some years ago in Rome
Wanted a date before I flew back home.
Where should we meet? We differed on that point.
He thought the station was a seedy joint –
Insisted on a more romantic place.
Beside the Tiber, by a statue's base,
I waited and I watched the river's flow –
You've guessed it, yes – the bugger didn't show.
Take my advice, a girl should never trust
The sentimental man. Just go for lust.

Though I am unromantic, I must say,
I like some cards upon St Valentine's Day.

Among my last year's crop two stand apart.
One from a maniac-fan had little art –
A pair of lips like Jagger's, inches wide,
Spanning the glossy card from side to side,
All heavy-breathed upon (or something worse . . .)
Inside, the usual Patience-Weak-type verse.
The other (nameless donor) was discreet,
With twenty quid in vouchers – *that* was sweet!

I like to send a card or two for fun,
Nothing too serious, like this year's one –
A model muscleman without a dong,
A life-size stand-up thing – it's six foot long.
All muscles, arteries and veins are there
Except a certain part's. It seems unfair
This Frankenstein of cardboard has no means
Of reproduction printed in his genes.
I'll send him with a message to a bard
Who led me on then spurned me good and hard.
I'll write: 'My lips are red, my blood is blue,'
And then, 'I've got no balls though – just like you!'

'Expense of Spirit'

'Shakespeare's a good psychologist' I'd said,
(the present tense, the man still lives to me) –
a casual remark, post-mortemised
by the historian I was talking to.
'He couldn't be – psychology's a science
that wasn't even invented in his day . . .
Shakespeare showed feeling for his fellow man!'
(He told me what he thought I'd meant to say.)
I felt the sofa wasn't long enough
for both of us and wished he'd go away.

OK, I know that Shakespeare wasn't a shrink
(more qualified in poaching than exams)
and didn't question people on his couch.
Or, if he did, he wasn't paid for it.
I still maintained that Shakespeare analysed
our motives for each act and wrote that truth.
Clever Dick challenged me to prove my point.
'One line' he ordered, 'or a part of one'.
A hundred things (and all irrelevant)
went coursing through my mind, like 'Out damned spot!',
'Then slip I from her bum; down topples she',
I settled for 'men have died from time to time
and worms have eaten them, but not for love'.
Mercifully, he went off to look it up.

Shakespeare wrote many thousand truths –
open the Works at almost any page.
(I sometimes use the book for oracles.)
The only line *I*'d quarrel with's on lust.

Come off it, Shakespeare, lust's a lot of fun.
Like meals, or visits to the theatre,
it's over soon, but leaves good memories.
If thwarted, there's less pain in it than love.
Lust is quite practical. (There's plenty more

fish in the sea – if what you fancy's fish.)
Love's complicated – the expensive one.
The thing unbalances, throws judgement out.
Its centring on one and only one
engrosses thought and permeates your life.
We writers, when in love, have twice the work –
rewriting all the damned self-pity out.
All right, I know that love's not terminal.
As a disease, I'd call it chronic, though –
it reoccurs and's hardly curable.
There's nothing to be gained from it, unless,
by some rare chance, it's equal on both sides.
Your line on lust, exactly sums it up . . .
'Expense of spirit in a waste of shame'.

Careers

I used to play a game when I was small –
to win you had to notch up sixty points,
first setting a proportion for yourself –
making a cocktail out of stars for fame,
pound signs for cash and hearts for happiness.
The first few times I went for stars and lost –
fame seemed the only thing worth hoping for.
Tired of my losses I soon realised
that twenty, twenty, twenty gave good odds;
I changed my tactics and began to win.

Till thirty I pursued the fame ideal,
writing all week, thinking of little else.

Once published I began the search for cash.
My life had broadened out – I fell in love
(Before if I was asked 'Your place or mine?'
I'd always opted 'Yours'. Now, 'yours' meant 'hers' . . .)
I *needed* somewhere I could call my own.
I fought for jobs, demanded higher fees,
and worked, demoniacally, spurred on by love –
started four novels all at once – it seemed
the only way to pull enough advance.
The novels didn't take. I got my cash –
ironically, it came from Poetry.

I'm slightly known and have my mortgage now –
but what of hearts? How many have I won?
I really can't include the nutty fans
who claim to be in love though we've not met.
The man I'd choose, if life had given me choice,
is married to a harpy, overworked –
has only time to love me *slightly* back.
(A partially-requited love's much worse
than none at all – it keeps you hanging on.)
I'd settle for being second in his life.

(The latest status symbol for a man's
a mistress with a cottage by the sea.)

Twenty stars fame and twenty pound signs cash.
Is it just greed that I want all the rest –
to have my cake and eat it and stay slim?
I've laughed at those who settled for a job,
so they can marry, have a family,
and yet expect to gain some writing fame
from dabbling with a poem at weekends.
Yet poets – real ones not amateurs –
back in the days when poets were all men
(well, almost all) had love – a wife and kids –
unless they died romantically and young.

Winning

At ten, I saw my teacher was a snob –
She thought a kid was an uncultured yob
Unless, that is, its parents could afford
To take it off for holidays abroad.
'France? Switzerland? Italy? Brittany?'
She asked around – a cultured litany
Until she got to Mumbles in my case.
'You went to *Wales*' – the look upon her face!
(Luggage travels, Miss O. Yes, even bags can fly –
Dubrovnik, Delaware, Deauville, Dubai . . .
But are they any better for the trip?
No, simply battered, with a busted zip.)

Having once done a course at the Sorbonne,
She thought she'd pass her little learning on
And teach us kids a smattering of French –
First, schooly words like blackboard, desk and bench,
A boring song, 'Un eléphant se trompe
Enormement!' it went and then a comp –
She ordered us to write down all the words
For insects, reptiles, mammals, fish and birds.
We had half term to finish off our list.
An opportunity not to be missed –
I combed through all the Fables of Fontaine,
Went through a dictionary and back again
(Aardvark to zebra, zebra to aardvark),
Confident if I worked I'd make my mark.
I logged the name of every single creature,
Hoping against all hope to please that teacher.

Hard work alone will not improve your lot –
Your face fits (or does not) and *mine* did not –
Poor, partly Welsh, a loser in her eyes.
The comp was cancelled and I got no prize.

If sex, race, class or poverty offends
You're not allowed to win – there's no amends.

31

Epistle to Dr Niven, Literature Director

Subtitled: Epilogue to the case of Helen Fiona Pitt-Kethley versus the Arts Council of Great Britain, heard at Westminster County Court, September 21st and 22nd, 1989.

'The only prizes she'd win are of the cattle-market variety' – words spoken about me by 'an Arts Councillor' according to the *Sunday Times* – 'Diary', June 18th, 1989.

'Judge not that ye be not judged', *Sermon on the Mount. Authorised version.*

I'm a prize cow, the Arts Council's declared –
That's not a joke – although I twice have bared
All my credentials to their judging team,
My books don't count like others', it would seem.

Niven, we met last autumn in the court –
Well, almost met. You didn't like my sort.
I took your measure on the witness-stand.
Three years before that day I had been banned
From trying for a bursary because
'Asian or Afro-Caribbean' was
A main requirement in the entrance rules.
(Are all Arts Council forms devised by fools?)
Against all common sense, rich Rushdie could
Apply while I could not, the way things stood.

Paternalism is subtle apartheid:
Brits are all Brits, whether they're black or white.
My cause, I felt, was just. The CRE
Agreed – they chose to pay the costs for me.

Day one – my work came under scrutiny.
I held my peace, no chance for mutiny,
While your QC asked you about my writing.
You tried to make your answers witty – biting.

You'd heard me once – more 'like a cabaret'
Than reading. (That's quite flattering, I'd say.)

What else had I done wrong? Ah yes, I've called
Myself a satirist. The word appalled
As satirists were men like Pope and Swift
And I, of course, was lacking their great gift.
Your last complaint was that I'd written verse
On my affairs. (Now wouldn't it be worse
If I'd done some on yours?) Sorry – a joke –
You haven't the looks for an illicit poke.
The cross-examination starts – you're asked
How I would fare another year. You basked,
Smoothed back your locks, paused artfully and said:
'She'll have a chance . . . *until* her work is read!'
I'll not submit again, I know the score.
You'll have to buy my books to read some more.

Justice seemed overwhelmed, drowned in the sands
Of bureaucratic bumf in lawyers' hands –
Arts Council minutes to the millionth power,
Forcibly read out, hour by painful hour,
Several rainforests' worth, all very dry.
The boredom threshold of a judge is high,
But some things are too much. The ponderous weight
Tipped down the scales and sealed my case's fate.
Five present witnesses ensured it done;
The sixth uncrossexamined, absent one
Helped most of all – a Margaret Drabble letter.
Judge Harris said: 'I couldn't have put it better!'
'The daughter of a judge,' he let us know
(In loving tones). His cheeks were all aglow.

Then it was verdict-time. We sat enthralled.
The summing up began and I was called
'Per-poetess' – the pejorative way
That word was said told me I'd lost the day.
As Dickens wrote, 'The Law's an ass' (in fact
It's worse – a donkey half as slow'd be sacked).

Niven, you know I had no chance, bound by
The Court's strict etiquette, for a reply.
The Law was far too formal, not much fun.
You want a fight, sir? Well, I'll give you one.
My barrister was much too nice a man
And lawyers can't stoop as low as satirists can.
I'll show my brotherhood with Swift and Pope –
As either would have done, I'll give you rope
To hang yourself. You've taken on the task
Of judging poems. Can *you* write one? I ask.
When those who can are judged by those who can't,
The abler poets seldom get a grant.
Some Civil Servants, jaded academics
Do manage to bash out pastiche polemics.
Are you that sort – a cultured bureaucrat,
Or just a Philistine and Führer-pratt?
I challenge you to a poetic duel,
And if you can't cough up a literary jewel
At least as good as this – well then, resign.
Your credibility is on the line.

Songs of Praise

I went and joined the throng in 'Songs of Praise'
'Stand up, sit down' for three hours in the sun.
The BBC knows well how to exploit –
free extras for the afternoon – you'd think
that they'd have mustered up some cups of tea,
turned water into wine, or better still,
dispensed some loaves and fishes through the crowd.
(Instead, the local council'd pitched its tent
to cash in quickly on religious thirst.)

I'd told myself that I liked singing hymns –
I used to years ago, when in the choir.
But now, I found their easy, stilted tunes –
verse following verse – no challenge musically.
My voice is more for singing solos now.
I sang the stuff about the 'love of God'
and felt nothing, this time, but emptiness.

A tramp dropped by in trunks and floppy hat,
put down his fish and chips, unwrapped some clothes
and pulled a pair of ancient trousers on
while all the Christian ladies looked askance.
(His voice was the best baritone for miles.)

That afternoon, with all its endless takes,
the boredom and the sunlight in my eyes,
the feeble jokes to keep us singing on,
put paid to all religion in my heart
and exorcised the last crumbs of their God.

For years, after I'd given religion up,
I'd find myself starting to pray again,
like some poor sucker doing his weekly pools
or polishing a Pixie amulet
seen in an ad in Old Moore's Almanack.
It never worked, even when I believed.
Whatever thing I asked for, small or large,

I never got. For me, religion's like
a slot machine where all the choc's run out.
However much I kick the thing and swear,
it won't deliver sweets. Old habits die hard.
I tried for far too long, but now I find
my senseless urge has absolutely gone.
I thank the BBC and 'Songs of Praise'.

Censorship

The BBC does not like certain words.
Dildoes and buggery are always out.
'Cocks are OK, as long as they aren't sucked' –
a young researcher telephoned me back.

Latin's polite. *Vagina* just meant *sheath*.
What doctors use, of course, must be all right.
(But *penis* was a *penis* – nothing else.
The Romans liked to call a prick a prick.)

The BBC's *De-effer* bleeps things out
or else suggests a synonym instead.
A poet I know was told he should use *screw* –
his line – 'There's fuck-all fucking in the grave.'

I got away with using bugger once.
I tried to be demure at first and said
it rhymed with Rum Tum Tugger, but the host
coerced me to recite it at the end.

In Wales, I said a simple 'prick' and 'piss' –
the show's producer had okayed both words –
but when the bosses' switchboard jammed with calls,
her earphone buzzed 'For God's sake, get her off!'

These days, when on the air, I just conform
and skirt around like the professionals,
so audiences can play a crossword game –
'Four letters, sounds like duck, begins with F.'

The Editor

Auschwitz and Belsen's victims turned him on –
the maimed, the scarred, the terminally thin.
His first erection happened spontaneously
while looking at a newsreel on TV.
I heard about this from a friend whose friend's
the Jewish girl he'd told this story to.

We've all enjoyed the thought of cruelty
when we were young and could not visualise
the painful horrors of the real thing.
At school, I know I laughed uproariously
on hearing of a martyr who had burst –
but I was only seven, with nothing erect.

Anti-semitic hard-ons should be kept
well-hidden beneath their pervert-owner's hats.
They're no fit subject for a boast to those
whose relatives, perhaps, died in those camps.

Fantasies, once recited out aloud,
become a tool to turn on, move or wound.

Mortal Clay

Who knows what's happening in the 'average' home?

A *Forum* reader writes to tell the world
about his special Christmas treat. He'd bought
two pots of Playdoh from his local shop,
pummelled the contents and then moulded it
inside the tallest glass that he could find.
Wetting the clay so that the thing'd feel right,
he wedged the glass between his parents' beds.
(His parents were away for the weekend.)
Pants down, he thrust into it, deep and hard,

This country's long male baby boom's lined up
a surplus of a million and a half.
Should be good news for women everywhere.
Statistics, though, show only partial truth.
Perhaps the million and a half young men
all prefer Playdoh cunts to human flesh.

Life Insurance

'You'll have no looks for picking up more men
by 60 . . .' I am warned.

I'm single, 35, and screw around.
These facts offend the average male.
I ought to settle down with one of them.

Can marriage bring security in age?
Loneliness cannot be insured against.

Warnings, like love, should be reciprocal.
'50 or 60, left without a mate,'
I like to caution those who've cautioned me,
'a fading, balding man whose wife's pissed off.
Tired of your quest for ever younger girls,
she takes a leaf out of your book
and finds herself an even younger man.'
A *woman's* potency is never gone.

Death on Film

If all the cowboys in a film were killed –
great, loping, bandy, bean-fed farting oafs –
who'd care? Not I. (Horses and dogs
touch me much more. *They* haven't asked for it.)

War heroes gunned by German officers
don't move me – cardboard men who'd just as soon
strap on a brace of artificial legs
get in a plane and bomb the other side.
(War heroes never learn that killing's wrong,
however many bits they've had shot off.)

And as for dying lovers – they're the pits.
They keep their photogenic, glossy looks,
while saying that they've something terminal –
tumours, leukaemia, cancer – take your pick.
For all such death-bed scenes, I would advise –
switch off, walk out, or vomit quietly.

The Birds and the Bees

Thirty per cent of fledglings in the nest
weren't sired by the male in residence.
Recent research has shown birds screw around –
yes, even good old swans and turtle doves!

A queen bee's even worse – one outing on,
she's scored with twenty-five of her doomed drones.

Beasts like a marriage of convenience –
they settle down, but go on playing the field.
The male is there to help bring up the kids –
or not, as in a tom cat's case. (He just
pops round to see all's right and's frequently
told to piss off in no uncertain terms.)

Farm animals, of course, have far less fun –
they serve and wait in segregated fields.
Their only copulation's once a year –
a stud's brought round for all of them, or worse,
the vet comes with his briefcase full of sperm.
Do cows enjoy the artificial bit?
Perhaps – but less than choosing their own bull.

If each male bird's a cuckold through and through,
and every beast, *by preference*, plays around,
should Man alone stand against Nature's trend?

You kiss a lot of frogs to find your prince
(or at the very least, a better frog).
Every important choice should be informed.
There's sense in that. But open marriages?
Swine may get fevered, cows go mad, but none
get clobbered with pox, clap or AIDS, unless
men give it to them in laboratories.
To take risks on your own is fair enough,
but not to ruin someone else's life.

If Fortune's wheel brings round a golden age
where sexual infections are not known
(as they weren't known in Ancient Rome or Greece)
and we could all do what the queen bee does,
or 'swing' like rabbits with impunity,
once all my oats were sown and I had found
my better frog, I'd opt for faithfulness.

Licensed adultery can only bring
the negative emotions to the fore –
wifewatching, voyeurism, jealousy.
Cuckolds of either sex become a joke.

Romance

I hate romance. I hate all Mills and Boon.
And Barbara Cartlands really make me sick.
I loathe the trash that people push as love.

A husband talks to me about his wife,
calls her 'a real bitch'. She sounds one too –
the sort you only can laugh at not with.
(Her jokes are purely practical.)

He closed the shutters, sat there opposite,
last time he called me round and told me that
the treatment had got worse. I wondered how.
(The trip before, I'd heard he'd come in tired –
she lay upon the sofa on a sheet.
He saw the writing on the wall beside –
her message for him – DEAD OF BOREDOM – scrawled
like blood in bright red paint across the white.)
He seemed to think *her* words could still be seen
beneath *his* several coats of vinyl matt.

Society pities the faithful wife,
the bruised and battered wife who waits at home
while hubby has his office-party screw.
Yet men who're knocked around are just a joke.
And he whose wife's a whore is thought a pimp.

I'm not society.
I'm really *really* sorry for this man –
right up until the moment that he says
he's stuck it all for love.

Love? Shit! that's abject masochism.

Her tapir's profile triumphs from the wall.
(He has to have pictures of her around.)
This one's surrounded by a glittering frame –

cemented shards of broken mirror-glass –
Madame de Sade, I think, probably made
him walk across them first.

One in Three

One in three marriages ends in divorce,
but not the ones that we most want to end.
Marriages are like kings in history –
the weakest are bumped off or forced to quit –
the really bad are left to do their worst.

Dad buggers little Sandra twice a week.
The social workers see they aren't split up –
he speaks them fair and goes for therapy.

'The sanctity of marriage' – what a joke!
Other things like children's welfare should come first –
divorce disturbs them, so does staying put
when there's abuse or violence in the home.
A battered wife (or husband) should walk out.

These days most people are content to move
at frequent intervals. They leave their home
and Mum and Dad to set up on their own,
pair up, then want a slightly larger place,
move South or North to get a better job,
have kids, go to the country for their sake,
then down the housing chain when they've moved out
and to some sheltered flat for their old age.
Why not treat marriages in the same way?

Some places grow untenable in time –
better a short lease on a rotten house.
Others just need a fortune spent on them.
Sometimes a property is simply wrong –
too old, too new for those who live in it.

I take my hat off to the one in three.

Citizens' Advice Bureau

I'm like the Citizens' Advice Bureau –
men gravitate to me for counselling.
I 'Mm', 'Oh dear!' and 'What a shame!' for them.

I'm 'understanding' men have often said,
which means they offload things about their wives,
their girlfriends or their stupid fantasies.

I'm really sick of it. I sit there thinking:
pick some unlucky vicar for this shit,
take out your pen, write the lot down, send it
to someone who is *paid* to understand –
Marge Proops, Claire Rayner, Irma Kurtz, *not* me.
Or, take your aberrations to a shrink –
at fifty quid an hour – so he can say
it's all because you want to have your mum.
With half the wimps I know, he might be right . . .

I'd tolerate *some* moans along the road.
A man who tells me that his wife's a bitch
is doing verbal foreplay of a sort.
(He means 'I'd like to trade the faggot in
for someone else like you, or at the least,
I feel that I deserve some light relief.')

The men who make me angry are the ones
who tell their tales like Ancient Mariners –
I'm forced to listen, forced to empathise.
They drain me, hardly leave me time for life –
time to develop problems of my own.
It isn't even foreplay with these types –
just an appalling kink that leads nowhere.
I'm tired of being used by useless men.
The only pleasant way to 'use' is sex –
it gives a chance to use the user back.

Unwanted confidences should be spilt . . .
I put the lot in poems, serve them right.

One of these so-and-sos of complaining men
used me for months (or was it years?)
Sympathy ought to be reciprocal –
one day, I felt I needed a kind word.
(Six pipes had burst; three of my ceilings fell.
I scooped up ten or twenty bucketfuls
of plaster lumps, stray lathes and sandy sludge,
shovelling and scraping it from sodden rugs,
burying it in a trench beneath the snow.
The sofa where I sprawl to write was soaked.
The typewriter was full, my newest work –
roughed in black ink – pulped to a soggy mess.)
I wrote a card, a plea for sympathy.
We met. He chose that day to finish things.

I took it rather badly at the time –
and hated him until he patched it up.
These days, I can acknowledge he was right
and handled friendship the courageous way.
Once I had troubles, I became a bore –
bores should be sacked. I wish I had his nerve.

Vultures

Cultured men torture writers for their kicks.
Boredom's their weapon – an effective one.
(Philistines are more fun to listen to.)
Inspired by some demonic anti-muse
they turn up on your doorstep well-equipped
to knock your latest poem on the head.
They stay for hours and when the bastards go,
we're hardly fit for anything at all.
The 'man from Porlock' perhaps started it
with nobbling Coleridge's Kubla Khan.

One of these vultures came to me last June –
in shirt and jacket on a summer's day.
He plumped himself down right by the table
like a bloke ordering his fish and chips.
'I've read some articles by you and thought
we ought to meet,' he said three times and smiled.
Conceit oozed visibly from every pore
(the day was hot). 'I could write articles!'
He could *perhaps*, but didn't – the reason why
the jerk had time to come and pester me.
He worked in 'a city bank', he explained,
at least – he had 'time off for some exams'.
Now, job descriptions are a sort of art –
bank clerk with breakdown, was my evil thought.
Of course, I could be wrong – perhaps he had
a Porsche and bimbos parked a street away.

If I should make a pile, when I am old,
perhaps I'll emigrate, seek solitude –
like Graham Greene in Antibes. But then,
I know the buggers would still come. In fact,
they'd come with suitcases and stay a week.

Entertaining

I don't like visitors. I meet my friends
in pubs where *others* do the washing-up.
A dinner-party's my idea of hell.
(Guests come to criticise, I've learned that much.)

All right – I compromise, and with a smile
provide drinks, coffee and a home-made cake
(when forced to it). But still I draw the line
at full-blown meals – the planning's difficult
like simultaneous orgasm – meat and veg.
rarely arrive together or on time.

Blow Jobs

You'd get more protein from the average egg;
the taste's a tepid, watery nothingness –
skimmed milk? weak coffee? puréed cucumber?

Fellation's not a woman's idea of fun.
Just doing it as foreplay is OK.
You kiss me, I'll kiss you's a quid pro quo –
but carrying on until the buggers come –
suck, suck, suck, suck for half a bloody hour!
(I haven't timed it but it feels that way.)

There's nothing in the act for us. Our mouths
are better stimulated by a kiss.
The sucked lie back (with beatific smiles),
forget our bodies in their private dreams,
while we grow cold, detached, unloved, untouched,
our heads like 3-D sporrans on their groins,
bored out of mind, with aching jaws and cheeks,
like kids that Santa gave a plastic flute,
still trying to get a tune on Boxing Day.

'Toothless George' sucked all comers to the rocks
in a secluded Jersey cove each June.
(He'd come from Blackpool for his yearly treat.)
Men love the act, sucking and being sucked.
Most women wish they'd keep it to themselves.

Condoms

I've searched the British Library for a verse –
'In Praise of Condoms' – that I'm told exists.
Dorset? Or Rochester? The great Anon?
I haven't found it yet – I'll write my own.

'In Praise . . .'? Not really, I don't like the things.
An older generation – mostly men –
can find eroticism in a pack,
remembering how they carried them in youth,
hoping for what they very rarely had.
My generation, brought up on the Pill,
now finds its freedom radically gone.

What does the donning of a rubber say?
I don't quite fancy you? Or trust myself?

Hygiene has routed pleasure in a world
where all the milk is thin and pasteurised
(except one or two sources that I've found),
where slimy, pissed-in public baths are thought
much safer for a swimmer than the sea,
where paranoia and disinfectant reign.

Now sex is cling-wrapped for security.
We plan and carry three packs in our bags
(nobody runs to six with condoms on).

Oral? *Or* intercourse? The two don't mix –
unless you get the order right – who wants
a mouthful of some poisonous spermicide?
Sex has become a shorter, drier act.
With something in between you both, there's not
much giving left. The condom keeps his sperms;
its friction strips the woman's lubricity.

I dream of a return to freer days . . .
What should I do – just risk those lethal germs?
I would if it were only for myself.
Sex with a condom's better than none at all –
that's true. Yet, their inhuman rubberiness
has almost made me feel like settling down.
I think I'd even tolerate romance –
simply to chuck the goddam things away.

Penetration

These days, non-penetrative sex is in
and good old-fashioned fucking's gone right out.
Fear's killing it. But why? A condom guards
both parties from much risk of a disease.
Men *also* fear that they won't measure up –
a finger is much easier to erect.

I'd opt for penetration, any day –
the other stuff is foreplay, to my mind.
Hands, fingers, toes, tongues, mouths can just provide
a pleasant interlude, hors d'oeuvres, perhaps.

Mutual masturbation's useful though –
a kindly sort of way to satisfy
(and rid ourselves of) someone slightly old,
or slightly worse in any other way
than those that we're accustomed to pick up.
We *really* fancy? Then we want *full* sex.

Tools

A prick's an under-rated sort of tool –
it's custom-built to do the job in hand.
They're changeable, it's true, but so's a Strad.
Some instruments simply require a tune.

Vibrators aren't a patch. Plastic's too hard
to bend the way a woman's passage bends.
Latex, though much more flexible, smells bad –
like red hot tyres and clapped out tennis shoes.
Aesthetically, you'd have to choose a cock –
the problem is the men by whom they're owned.

Equality

Some argue feminists shouldn't like a fuck.
The fact that men are oftener on top
is taken metaphysically. They're seen
as dominating while the woman submits.
Like Hell! That's what they think . . .

You feel abused? A door mat underneath?
The answer's simple – change it all around –
roll over, get on top and milk him dry.

There's a third path, where neither dominates.
Why don't we settle for equality –
my favourite way – and do it side by side?

Bed Time

Sex in the afternoon is always good –
it's honest lust, not lodgings for the night –
no one's too drunk or tired to manage it.

The afternoon's discreet, ambiguous,
a time when no excuses need be made.
Each enjoys each – they know as they are known.
There's no concealment – daylight's always on.
And when it's time to leave, the night's still young –
home, food, TV all wait – and best of all,
the peace of being alone in your own bed.
Solitary sleep's less disillusioning.

Night sex is often far less pleasurable –
a tired, furtive, fumbling in the dark.
Objective vision comes with morning's light.
(I have the knack of always waking first.)
I dreamed of friends but find a stranger there –
his mouth gapes snoring wide; yesterday's style –
the careful, blow-dried cut – is now on end;
one duvet-clutching hand has dirty nails;
and, something ludicrous, the modest sod's
managed to get his pants back on in bed.
He wakes and things get worse. I must wipe off
the grin those pants inspired and try to talk.

The in-built problem with a one-night stand
is how to handle things after you've slept.
How many lovers' moods are synchronised?
An early-morning surliness in one
undoes everything tender done or said.
I'd advocate pre- or post-breakfast fucks
to show continuance of last night's desire –
proof positive that neither has regrets.

No Smoking

Lent is the time for cutting out what's bad,
I'll give up going to bed with men who smoke –
for that *and* other seasons of the year.

Is it the taste? That's not *too* bad as long
as I don't put my tongue into their mouths.
The tiredness of their skin? Their blood-shot eyes?
Is it the smell of fag-ash in my hair
next day? Not really. That can be washed out.

Post-coital light-up is what worries me.
We've had each other, then the smoking man
turns desperately seeking something else,
scouring the bedside cupboard, pockets, drawers.
He sighs on finding what he really wants,
then's silently unfaithful with his fag.

Some keep their little weapons to themselves.
The worst kind start a sort of troilism.
I don't feel easy with a naked flame
too near my vulnerable naked flesh –
you, me, a cigarette, a smoky kiss.
Out of the corner of one eye I see
a toppling inch of ash above a stub,
while lover-boy is fiddling with my tits –
foreplay designed to set the bed on fire.

Notes to the Poems

Notes to the Poems

The 'notes' in *The Perfect Man* excited a lot of comment from friends and enemies alike. People wondered if I *really* received such letters. Yes, I do. Sometimes I even get gifts with them – anything from bath oil to condoms. I sent the condoms back in case the devil had been at them with a pin. There's something very unattractive about a pack with one missing and no Sell By date.

By popular request, I shall be including a few more of these letters – even one from Sir Francis Drake – at the end of these notes.

The more romantically inclined send me poems – I am beginning to have quite a collection of these. A brief selection of them appears with the letters, including an infuriated reply by *The Perfect Man* who had read my poem about him and decided to strike back. Unfortunately his spelling was not as perfect as he thought. Anyone wishing to abuse a writer should check it all out with a dictionary beforehand.

Notes to *Birdwatching*

The following article has proved to be the most popular I have ever written. Wherever I go, seagull-fanciers home in on me, saying: 'I cut out your article and kept it, I've got one on my roof too.' Strangest of all, someone from the Bristol BBC rang me at the time, wanting to crawl around my roof recording their dawn chorus. I said yes, with some trepidation, knowing it might mean a five o'clock start. He then went on to tick me off, as if I was the mother bird, for allowing my chicks out of the nest so early. Fortunately, I did not hear from him again. I have always imagined he meant to recontact me, but fell off somebody else's roof in the meantime. I have since tried to get myself hired by a paper as a nature columnist, on the grounds that I might do it more racily, than the average old-vicar type, but nobody's bitten yet.

Slightly longer version of my *Independent* article

One of the pleasures of living in Hastings is watching the gulls. In recent years they have become thoroughly urbanised and now picket restaurants looking for Big Macs and Kentucky Nuggets. They also come and knock on your bedroom window if you sleep at roof level. Sometimes, when I see a pair of benign straw-coloured eyes peering through the panes, I am not quite sure who is watching whom. My first knocker was a big male bird. I christened him Hugo, after a friend. For the first few weeks I assumed his intentions were merely voyeuristic until it dawned on me that he was begging. After several months of regular feeds at dawn, he started to bring his mate round. I called her Fifi. You can tell a female seagull because they are smaller, with thinner necks and sweeter, higher voices.

Gulls are like Hoovers for most foods, although they do draw the line at salad or high fibre stuff. Unless there's a foot of snow and they're desperate, they won't touch my home-made stoneground bread. A nice white junky cracker is more in their line. Their favourite food is cheese, so they sometimes get a cube or two to finish off passed round like the After Eights. Male birds will take food from your hand once they know you. The females aren't allowed to – they have to hang about, one step behind their lord and master. The more you get to know gulls, the more like humans they seem. A spiritualist in the local sauna told me they were the spirits of sailors. These days I can even seem to hear them scream odd English words (in a marked Cockney accent). The females complain bleakly with three-note cries that sound remarkably like 'Feed me please' or 'Give me some'. If they're good – i.e. properly subservient – they get a few scraps the male has trodden on plus a spot of mouth-to-mouth regurgitation.

I see evidence though of the beginnings of a war of the sexes. Female Gulls' Lib is on its way. Fifi is subtle about it. She sometimes turns up half an hour before dawn for the goodies. She doesn't risk any plaintive cries, but does one quick knock on the glass with her beak. Half an hour later she comes back standing meekly behind Hugo. He looks surprised there's not as much as usual.

Mating occurs in spring. You can see them having a high old time on all the roofs and chimneys. Perverser gulls do it on skylights. The female gets things going with a softer, cooing version of 'Feed me please' and 'Give me some!' She stays with her partner as long as he protects the eggs properly – a lifetime if he's lucky. If he slips up, then it's off to some other roof for a toy boy. The nests are more of a token gesture than a proper home – just a few bits of straw, seaweed and refuse like crabs' claws.

Last year there were the usual mating rituals, but few birds had young. Local councillors who call for culls, assuming every pair of birds will breed a pair every single year, are ignoring natural wastage. Probably there was too much roofing work going on in the aftermath of the hurricane for the eggs to survive. Gulls and roofers are sworn enemies. The birds are often thought aggressive, but in practice, they are only so when they feel their eggs are threatened. Roofers have to work in pairs in the summer. When working near a nest, one man has to field off birds with a scaffolding pole to protect his mate. Unfortunately some men tease the birds, trying to see how near they can make them dive. One man showed my mother a nasty scar on his neck from an attacking bird.

Gulls are good parents. The males have the decency to take it in turns minding the eggs. For the weeks that follow mating I get only one bird coming across at a time. When their little monsters are hatched the parents become desperate for extra food. Young herring gulls wheeze asthmatically for food, twenty-four hours a day. You can see their parents knitting their brows with the worry of it all. When the birds are old enough to fly, they come across too. By then, they are adult-size. I nickname these birds 'loobies' – a sort of Scots dialect word for big young brainless oafs. They look like an entirely different breed. They are speckled brown with black beaks and sloe-like eyes that fill with an expression of pain and reproach if you don't provide food immediately. They also have long wrinkled legs like St Trinian's stockings, large brown leather feet and a very low IQ. Their elders and betters have to get them out of scrapes endlessly as they climb TV aerials, stand for hours gazing at their reflections in puddles or drop four storeys into the street on kamikaze flights. Parents put in a lot of time on flying lessons. I like to think that the females are better at it. They demonstrate subtle, perfectly-timed figures of eight round the local roofs. The males are more into staccato flights and snatch-and-grab raids. The young usually start by running awkwardly down steep roofs shrieking wildly. They seem to fear flight as much as we do. They are not naturals at it. They have to learn. There's an interesting solidarity between the gulls on the block. When a youngster does his first successful solo flight they all break into joyful cries – 'He can fly! He can fly!'

My first visiting loobie I called Sonny Jim. He was particularly partial to snacks of mussels which I acquired while going to the beach for a daily swim. He used to stand back and wait while I smashed them open for him with a hammer. Sometimes, when I went upstairs, I found him in the small kitchen next door to my bedroom, ready and waiting. I'd shout 'You! Out!' to him and he usually understood. One day though, I had to hiss to make him leave. We were never as good friends after that.

By the autumn, the young gulls are usually off and away. They don't change their plumage completely for five years. I suppose that they spend much of their time travelling until then. The parents keep on coming across on their regular pitches. The man opposite me talks of giving two very hungry birds breakfast, tea and lunch in his garden. They may well be my two.

Not content with all he can gather from my road, Hugo goes down the tip. He comes back with very dirty feet and occasional bouts of food-poisoning. He's a handsome bird normally, but gets swollen with slitty eyes at times like that. Fifi looks after him then and manages his begging round. He had a near scrape last year when he came back with the plastic rings off a four-pack stuck in his mouth and round his throat like a terrible sort of scold's bridle that was gradually strangling him. He resisted my attempts to creep up behind him with scissors and sat it out for a week in the angle behind the roofs opposite. He spent hours every day rubbing it against the tiles with Fifi mounted guard on a chimney above him. Then he would go to sleep in a heap with sheer exhaustion. Eventually his perseverance worked and he was free. Those four-packs have been the end of a lot of seagulls. Mindful of that, I cut through the plastic now before I throw the bits away.

This year another pair have joined the regular call. They are not a typical seagull couple. Freckles is a far less noble bird than Fifi. She knocks poor Flat-top around. Worse still, she has even been known to walk up and over his back, then grab food from his beak. He takes it all very well. If both couples turn up at the same time there are usually quarrels. The males bite the backs of each other's necks and the females advance on each other saying 'Ninininini' in a sort of timid defiance. It's all pretty much like the average party of lager louts at closing time. I just let them get on with it and don't take sides.

Almost every year, some holidaymaker complains to my local paper about my friends, the gulls. This year I sprang to their defence under an assumed name:

Dear Editor,

On behalf of myself, my wife and two young sons may I say I was disgusted by the contents of Fred Thompson's anti-gull letter (August 8). Does he really want to bring his children up in a world without birds? The way some humans are carrying on, that may well be a future possibility. I have lost a good many friends under the wheels of cars and to oil-slicks.

Mr Thompson seems to ignore our tireless work for the community, carrying off unwanted fish heads from the beach, not to mention the packets of chips, half-eaten baked potatoes, sandwiches, Big Macs and chewed-up pizzas that his kind drop around the town. We are also prepared to pose for photographs. More discerning visitors describe us as a tourist attraction. Some residents even find us inspiring. Fiona Pitt-Kethley has written a poem about us, and Laetitia Yhap has drawn and painted us many times.

Some of my gull-friends – mostly those who've seen a certain Hitchcock film – have suggested that we mount an attack on Mr Thompson. Personally, I believe in the sanctity of other forms of life – even the lowest ones. I would even wish to spare Mr Thompson's children, although they spoiled many a good siesta for me as they 'screeched, honked, mewed or clacked' the whole afternoon through beneath the roof I have inhabited for years.

A. Gull (long-term resident of St Leonards)

Note to *Valentines* and *Long-Stemmed Rose*
The six-foot-long card sent to the bard mentioned at the end of *Valentines* was a 'Three-Dimensional Man'. I had received the same as a joke Christmas present while appearing on a pilot for the *Behind the Headlines* show.

David, the hero of *Long-Stemmed Rose*, and the sender of the luscious-lips card mentioned in *Valentines*, pestered me with a ten-page letter a day for many weeks and worse still, threatened to spend Christmas with me, whether I liked it or not. Eventually, I got rid of him by pretending I had a full-time boyfriend. It's a lie I sometimes have to use – men are considerably less willing to accept that I simply don't fancy them. Here is David's final letter:

Dearest Fiona,

What a pity some people, rather like you, can only see their own noses and do not meant to see the good solid wood for the trees.

Your letter apparently saying goodbye makes me more angry than sad for you are throwing yourself into an affair which even though it may come to something at the present time will only end in divorce.

You cannot go by a persons face and as for likeing a person only for his so called attractive 'face' is just another farce in the series of idiotic acts that so far have made up your whole existence.

When you suddenly decide that love and true warmth, something you have obviously never known, is more

66

important than relationships with 'children' aged between 24 and 34 whose only appeal to you is the face, then I shall be waiting for you.

Albeit I shall have, at the moment to wait in the wings like some actor waiting for his cue to a triumphant entry.

But my dear Fiona, my Pyrrhic Victory will be soon, sooner than you think.

Faces don't count for a thing, one can have the most handsomest face in the world and a rotten character underneath. Beware your so called present 'friend' isn't the same.

I give it six to eighteen months and that is a hell of a long time.

Yours as always David.

Notes to *Epistle to Dr Niven*

In '89 I took the Arts Council to court for racial discrimination, funded by the Commission for Racial Equality. In some ways I have since regretted doing this – not because I believed for one minute I was wrong – but because, when a case is *sub judice* you find that your freedom to talk about it has gone. Probably I could have fought the Arts Council better if I'd stuck to satirising them.

Fuller version of my report on the case for the Independent
Going to court is an occasion for sartorial restraint. In the world of wigs, gowns and judges who might take exception to women who wear trousers, you have to get it right. I donned my barrister-type black suit (vintage 1940s) and a discreet beige silk blouse. I also sprinkled on the Blue Grass talc in the hopes that the judge might consider me 'fragrant'. He didn't.

In '86, I had got to the stage professionally where I felt I would have a very good chance if I applied for an Arts Council grant. I had achieved some fame with my first book of poems, but was earning little – about £2,000 a year at that time. In theory I would have been an ideal recipient for an award. I wrote and asked for details in the summer and was told that there would be grants for poets that year and I would be sent an entry form. As no form arrived, I rang the literature department on 18th November and was told that grants that year were only open to 'Asian and Afro-Caribbean applicants'. I wrote suggesting this was discrimination and asked to be allowed to apply, but that cut no ice. After this I wrote a further letter on the subject to the Commission for Racial Equality. They decided to fund me in suing the Arts Council for racial discrimination. The Commission, it turned out, had not been consulted before the all-black bursaries were arranged. The only black member on the Arts Council's Literature Panel, Dr David Dabydeen, had voiced objections to limiting the grants to black applicants, but these had been ignored. Almost three years later, the case of Helen Fiona Pitt-Kethley versus the Arts Council of Great Britain came to trial on September 21st and 22nd at Westminster County Court.

I brought the case in the first place partly because of my own frustration at not being allowed to try for an award, and partly because I felt the Arts Council had ignored the success story of black literature. There are many black writers who have won major prizes in open competition, Anglo-Indian writing has been a thriving tradition for a surprising 150 years. I also felt that the Racial Discrimination Act should work both ways. A law about race discrimination that doesn't work for all races is essentially prejudiced and patronising. The Commission presumably felt this when they supported me. If a black person is to be truly an equal citizen, then he or she must stand exactly the same chance – neither more nor less – than a white person. That rule must be applied throughout employment, education and the social services. Logic demands nothing else.

I had never attended a court before and had little idea what to expect. By the end of the first day I realised that it was going to be more a case of *Rumpole of the Bailey* than *LA Law*. I take my hat off to John Mortimer for his realism, but I deplore the system. If the wigs and gowns were thrown out and everyone could sit round a table and discuss matters openly and freely, justice could be done with a lot more common sense, speed and less waste of public money.

The process continued to remind me of *Rumpole* as my

counsel, Kuttan Menon, and the Arts Council's QC competed in the old game of who could laugh hardest at the judge's jokes – 'Salman Rushdie? Oh, we'd better not mention that name too much here.' The curious truth about the Arts Council's adverts for awards is that Salman Rushdie, rich as he is, could have applied for one in 1986, but I could not.

On the 22nd September, the day that Kazuo Ishiguro was nominated for a Booker Prize, Judge Harris gave his summing up. The crux of it was that, yes, I had been discriminated against, but this was not unlawful because the Arts Council had succeeded in his eyes in proving that black people had special needs which had to be met.

I am still convinced that I was the victim of discrimination; I am not however convinced by the Arts Council's arguments. The documents lodged by the defendants were weighty in quantity rather than quality. The judge lifted his wig and mopped his head many times – and who could blame him? The Arts Council's 'Proposals for Developments' in the 'Ethnic Arts' contained many emotive quotes: 'The black-spots in England's inner cities are festering and dangerous. To let them rot would be inhumane; the recent riots suggest that it would also be dangerous . . .' A claim was made that because of lack of support for Asian and Afro-Caribbean Arts 'there were signs throughout the country, and particularly in London, that this issue was reaching explosion point'. 'Afro-Caribbean and Asian communities' were also referred to – whatever these are. I have news for the Arts Council. Most black people – in my generation at any rate – were born here and have equal status and equal rights as British citizens. Many live in posh areas of London, or as I do, in the South of England – to quote the two I've met most recently: Grace Nichols lives in the genteel town of Lewes, James Berry in Brighton. As to the 'explosion point' problem – well, most artists feel like that when we think of the Arts Council. Poet Jeremy Reed's reaction to my case was typical of that of many friends, 'Wish I could think of something to sue them for!' Arts Council inanities annoy all but those who serve on that august body – and, perhaps, Judge Harris. One of the most recent follies was advertising literary grants for children's authors, one of whom had to write books for children aged from '0 to 9'. Unless wombs have electric light installed, I should imagine that children of 0 would have a few problems reading them. Another condition of those awards was that writing should be 'for or about the multi-cultural society'. Beatrix Potter wouldn't have stood a chance unless rabbits are an ethnic minority.

The Arts Council is aiming at the moment to spend 4% of its budget on the 'ethnic arts' to reflect the 4% of the population that's black. That sounds fair until you dig deeper. My barrister sought to gain a definition of the phrase 'ethnic arts' from an Arts Council witness. ('Ethnic arts' is the 'in' term at the moment, because the phrase 'Black Arts' might have another construction.) Could 'ethnic arts' include the wonderful singing of Jessye Norman and Booker-winning novelists like Rushdie (or for that matter Anita Desai)? Unfortunately Judge Harris put a stop to my barrister's line of questioning. If high-profile black artists were not included in the documents produced by the Arts Council, then the statistics in them were misleading. If the phrase 'ethnic arts' only covers things like Indian Dance, Steel Bands, Dub Poetry and All-Black Theatre, then a larger proportion than that pretended is being spent on work by Africans, Caribbeans and Asians, because a good many people from these nationalities are involved in opera, art, classical theatre and literature. Opera houses, theatres, some magazines and the Poetry Society are all known as 'Revenue Clients'. If revenue clients spend some of the money the Arts Council gives them on black artists, the percentage is pushed higher than that given in the representations to the judge. In the case of literature, mainstream publishers – who may also be revenue clients – publish black writers. The Poetry Society, a revenue client, has black poets giving readings and has employed them as competition judges. Perhaps the Arts Council's whole argument – that it was suddenly necessary to spend the 4% of the literary budget constituted by the bursaries because *nothing* was being spent on black artists – could have been made to collapse if the judge had allowed my barrister to continue this important line of questioning in some detail.

The Arts Council called six witnesses – poet James Berry, publisher Margaret Busby, Deputy Secretary-General of the Arts Council, Anthony Everitt, Pippa Smith, a past employee, Dr Alastair Niven, the Literature Director and Margaret Drabble (by letter). Dr Alastair Niven was the only one I could feel moved to dislike as he made what seemed a gratuitous attack, from the witness box, on my validity as a poet. (His words are noted at greater length in the poem. It was at that stage, knowing I could not answer back in court, that I decided to write an epistolary satire to him.) Dr Niven and Roger Garfitt of the original panel that decided on the black-only awards were both instrumental in turning my work down for the next year's bursaries *after* I had lodged the case. If Fiona Pitt-Kethley tries for an award in the future, Dr Niven said, 'She will have a fair chance of one . . . *until* her work is read.' His words had a similar ring to something I had read in the *Sunday Times* 'Diary' on June 18th. Someone had leaked the story of the case and some words about me from 'an Arts Councillor' were added: 'I'm afraid the only prizes she'd win are of the cattle-market variety.'

The last witness was definitely the judge's favourite – two pages from Margaret Drabble. He spoke reverentially and lovingly of her being 'the daughter of a judge'. Her words were allowed to be read in court even though my side had been given no chance to reply and Ms Drabble was absent in Canada and could therefore not be cross-examined. Judge Harris quoted part of her words again at a later stage: 'I couldn't have put it better myself!'

I am depressed that this verdict will set a precedent. The Arts Council has licence to do it again. Other similar bodies may feel they have carte blanche to advertise grants or positions for black applicants only, as long as they can come up with at least a hundred pages of bumf on the 'special needs' of ethnic minorities. Nor will these documents have to contain precise statistics on the subject.

There are other factors in this precedent that ring alarm bells in my mind. Just who will be included in the 'African, Caribbean and Asian' writers as some of the advertise-ments phrased it? In the interest of picking nits while cross-examining me, the QC played with this definition and seemed to think that it could also include Turks and Israelis. (Bit unfair considering they can also try the Eurovision contest!) At a later stage the definition was considered to include white South Africans. Come back, Zola Budd, all is forgiven. If you've gone off running, how about writing an autobiography? The Arts Council plans to sponsor the well-paid field of biography next year. I'm sure they would love to give some money to an African. Or how about a South African white politician or two? They must have some memoirs to sell.

It seems to me that if the Arts Council wishes to continue limiting its grants to these nationalities only, the government will have to pass a new law, taking a leaf out of South Africa's books. All British citizens will need an identity card or passport to prove exactly what their ethnic origin is. I am not quite sure how this works in practice with those of mixed parentage. As a student I was friends with Omar Ebrahim, who has since made a name as an opera singer. He once jokingly confessed to being a mixture of Zulu, Hottentot, Indian, Italian and Welsh. Would his European mother's blood have debarred him from trying for an Arts Council grant? Like most of the black artists of my generation he was well-educated. He succeeded young as he deserved to do. A similar case is Fred d'Aguiar, a bright young Guyanese poet (with a little Portuguese blood) who is under 30 and has published two collections with Chatto and Windus — certainly more than most white poets have achieved by his age. I fail to see that either of these black artists had special needs. Some black writers are not too literate or educated, we had heard in court, and are afraid to fill in Arts Council forms. Come to think of it I've met a lot of white would-be bards like that, but I'm not too sure they deserve to be encouraged.

After reading the *Sunday Times* snippet which heads *Epistle to Dr Niven*, one of my fans retorted in rhyme:
    And whilst he waited, amidst the stress,
    An Arts Councillor wrote, without finesse,

In the *Sunday Times*, a jaundiced mess,
Of FPK, the 'sex-obsessed poet . . . ess?'

Her prize, they maintain, is only for cattle,
For best breed, I assert, without any battle,
Is the obvious retort to this tittle-tattle,
From that misguided snake, without but a rattle.

An issue of *Poetry Review* carried an article by me, *Advice to a Young Poet*, which mentioned Dr Niven's remarks in court about my work. In the next issue he made the following reply:

Dear Sir,

I am not surprised that Andrew Motion once asked Fiona Pitt-Kethley if her poems about male organs were true (Vol. 80 No. 3). In the absence of encountering whoppers in the opposite sex she tells quite a few herself. She completely misquotes me in the court case she brought against the Arts Council last year – which she lost hands down, as you might say – and says she will not be able to apply for an Arts Council bursary while I am a judge. I am not a judge, so Ms Pitt-Kethley may apply on exactly the same terms as anyone else. She is welcome to low cow-like through my letter-box to catch my attention, as she threatens to do, and I hope I will realise that she is not just reading one of her poems on the doorstep.

Yours sincerely,
Dr Alastair Niven
Director of Literature
Arts Council

I replied as follows:

23.3.91.

Dear Editor,

I must correct a couple of grave factual errors in Dr Niven's letter in response to my article on the poetry world. He writes 'in the absence of encountering whoppers in the opposite sex she tells quite a few herself'.

He is wrong on both counts. I have indeed encountered quite a few 'whoppers' in, or rather on, the opposite sex – none of them belonged to A. Niven, however. He is also incorrect about my telling whoppers, i.e. lies. Why would I need to when there are men like him to satirise?

Readers of this correspondence may be interested to know that I have challenged Dr Niven to a poetic duel in a poem which is to appear in *Bête Noire*.

Yours sincerely,
Fiona Pitt-Kethley

(The poem referred to in the last paragraph of my letter is of course *Epistle to Dr Niven*.)

Notes to *Mortal Clay*
The virgin who wrote the letter to *Forum* referred to in this poem was at least young. His chief folly, I suppose, was in boasting of the episode to its readers. The phenomenon of the male virgin is quite common, contrary to popular belief. Several have written to me. In the interests of promoting an understanding of the species I will give a brief portrait of one of my latest regular correspondents.

Mel, a middle-aged virgin, likes the *Sport* newspapers and takes photos. In the last paragraph of one long letter, he hoped that I might have friends who'd pose for him:

FIONA HAVE YOU ANY FRIENDS WHO MAY WANT TO BE MODELS
THEY MUST STRIP OFF THEIR CLOTHES, MAYBE USE A DILDO OR
ANY VEG LIKE CARROTS, CUE, OR A BANANA. HAVE SOME PICS OF

A GIRL WITH A LEAK THINK I TOLD YOU SHE PUTS IT UP HER
TWAT. WELL FIONA WILL END NOW AS WANT TO PLAY WITH MY
PRICK & SPUNK OFF. TAKE CARE DON'T FORGET MY BOOKS.

LOTS OF LOVE YOURS
TRULY
MEL XXXX CUNT

Mel was so impressed by the incident of the girl with 'THE
LEAK' that he told me the story in two letters. Mel is a
Welshman. He signed his first letter 'X TO YOUR CUNT'. This
shortened in later letters to a varying number of Xs and CUNT,
almost as if it was his surname. His envelopes bear the
mysterious logo, 'P.P.R.L.F.' – mysterious, that is, until he told
me that it stood for, 'PLEASE POSTMAN RUN LIKE FUCK'.
    Mel's only short letter came with a packet of condoms, one
missing:

DEAR FIONA

FOUND THESE FRENCH LETTERS NOT USED THOUGHT I WOULD
HAVE USE FOR THEM AT A SEX SHOW WITH MY EX-FRIEND BUT ITS
ALL OFF SO THOUGHT YOU MAY LIKE THEM WHEN YOU GO AWAY.
HAVE GOT ONE FOR NEXT MONTH IF I FUCK THIS GIRL DOUBT IT
WOULD MOST LIKE HAVE THROWN THESE AWAY AS THEY'RE
ONLY GOOD FOR END OF YEAR DREAMPT I WAS FUCKING YOU
LAST NIGHT, HOPE YOU HAVE SOME GOOD FUCKS

MEL. XXXX CUNT

Notes to *Condoms*
Being unable to locate *In Praise of Cundums* in respectable
volumes like Granger's *Index of Poetry*, I wrote to a Professor
friend of mine for advice. He came back with a more precise
title, *Panegyrick Upon Cundums*, and what might be the first
few lines: 'Happy the man, who in his pocket keeps,/Whether
with green or scarlet ribband bound,/A well-made cundum,'
etc. Armed with his letter headed 'University of California'
as an alibi, I implored the British Library staff for help. Was
there an index of seventeenth-century first lines, I asked. A

rather nice, churchgoing-type of lady agreed to put out a search on the internal computer for me. We wrestled for some half an hour, devising ever more devious archaic mispellings of condoms and panegyricks, but to no avail. Some weeks later, after I'd written my own version, I came on the original poem (or another on the subject, as the Professor's first lines were somewhere in the middle and in quotation marks). It was tucked away amongst anonymous bits and bobs in the back of a volume of Rochester's poems. I have included an extract from it in my *Literary Companion to Sex*.

Last words by fans and enemies
I received the following after writing a piece on obscene phone callers:

Dear Fiona,

When I read your 'Gentleman Callers' piece in *Forum*, I couldn't resist writing in to say what an interesting feature.

And also, you strike me as a very exciting person. I don't know how your love-life is at present, but I would love to offer you something more satisfying than just a chat on the phone.

First. I am clean and free from infection. Very much the same age and height as Michael Caine, but not so dissipated-looking.

My track record is good – nine out of eleven past partners rated me the best man ever in their lives (the other two wouldn't consider me as a man but just said I made a lousy husband).

While I try to get my first novel published, I work in the Civil Service to earn a crust meanwhile.

So let's meet over a snack or a drink and see what we think of each other.

Yours sincerely,
John.

(The same day I also received a letter from another *Forum* reader (a lecturer). He offered at some length to make me a dirty phone call at a time, and on a subject chosen by myself.)

Some letters come with photographs. Neale even sent me a photocopy of a snap of himself reclining with legs apart and cock rampant, together with the following letter:

Dear Miss Pitt-Kethley,

I'm sorry to bother you but I've wanted to go to bed with you since seeing your humpable body in a *Sunday Times* article a couple of years back.

As you can see I'm no Charles Atlas. Neither am I a stallion – more of a shetland pony.

I won't bore you with the ritual incantations of what I'd like to do. If you fancy me drop me a line and we'll sort something out. I'll get a saver return down to St Leonards and we could have a good fuck one afternoon.

If I've offended you please accept my apologies.

Best wishes
Neale XX.

Some letters are more consciously amusing:

Dear Fiona,

Have just read your brilliant book *The Perfect Man* after finally finding it at the library, amongst Gay Fiction and Teenage Romances.

I first read *Sky Ray Lolly* after my girlfriend showed me an article on you in the *Mail on Sunday – You* Magazine.

We were pleased to read about someone with the same attitudes especially 'one afternoon stands'!

You can spot us walking around Hastings. I'm the one with the bouffant black hair, too much mascara, and Jane's the one with a mini skirt and blue hair. Anyway hope you write more books.

Yours faithfully,
Matthew and Jane.

Or:

A complimentary letter, only, Miss Pitt-Kethley. You've become the toast of an East End pub! Is there any other contemporary poet/ess who can so charm a collection of ex-jailbirds, barrow-boys, duckers-and-divers and a vet (not me – I'm a univ. lecturer, Eng-Lit) that, having seen – and passed round the bar – your excellent poems in the *LRB* ('mikes yer fink mite!' the ex-jailbird said to me) they cry out for 'More!' So tonight I'll take 'em in *The Perfect Man*. Good! Your photograph is on the back, too, and your lovely face will charm them even more – and surprise the wankers!

'Cor, if this is poetry, wish we'd 'ad more of it at school!' one of the Kray family's friends said. I agreed with him. You've opened the eyes of the Blind Beggar – so congrats!

A fan (male I fink!)

Some letters are not as complimentary about my appearance – the following may have been meant to be a poem:

Dear Fiona,

I find your work funny, sexy and spunky
although I'm a little disappointed
that you're so damn ugly
(did you really fuck all those men?)
or was it just an unflattering pose?

Love
Andrew X.

Deeply annoyed, I answered on an open postcard, in the hopes that it would get him into trouble with his wife or mother, as the case might be:

Dear Andrew,

Yes, I really did . . . but you will not be joining their number. Most men think the picture on my book an

78

attractive one, but then, I suppose, *if* you're more into kids or men's backsides, a good-looking woman might not be your scene.

Fiona Pitt-Kethley.

David Vickery of *Late Night Late* (TVS) allowed me to read *Big Pricks* (from *The Perfect Man*) during an interview with him. Surprisingly, the same poem was later censored, or rather, vetoed by Craig Raine when John Whitworth tried to include it in *The Faber Book of Blue Verse*. After an interview, David Vickery received the following letter:

Dear David,

I have written twice to Graham Rogers and he has ignored me twice. I am writing to you to say that I was surprised at seeing at about 1am a Fiona Pitt-Kethley orating a couple of shall we say different sort of poems. I am not in the least offended but was surprised. I thought I was dreaming and hearing/seeing things but it was live and I did see and hear it.

I do not sleep only 20 minutes for about 3 times during the night or day I do not really sleep just rest for these 20 minute rest periods.

I would appreciate it if you could let Miss?? Fiona Pitt-Kethley have this letter which I have enclosed with the letter I sent to you.

I would describe myself definitely as a insomniac, but also a introverted ego-eccentric anchorite who is waiting for someone preferably a woman to get me out of my shell and be a extrovert. I am healthy, happy, never gets physically angry, only vocal threats but beware the Fire Dragon thats my name I designated myself, as I was born on the last day of the Cat (so I have 9 lives to live) just before the beginning of the year of the extravagant clever emperorial Dragon (Chinese Horoscope) I was nearly a leap year baby born in month of February so I am also a Pisces (a great lover) as well as a great thinker.

I am always helping other people with their problems

79

but it seems they only waste my time trying to fool and take from me, and use me for their own end, but I am not the fool they think I am, I am still free, I am the one and the only me, and always will be the one and only me!

Like I said earlier I am a bit eccentric, and I have a very strong will-power, and never will any one beat me or use me as they did in the past. *Like your strange word-Questions.* I must stop rambling, I am good at playing the fool, but I always get what I want eventually money and property does not worry me because in life the most precious (better than gold or platinum) thing is life itself and to be happy healthy and rich in love (not greed) which one day I will be. I am in a bit of a STATUS QUO at the moment (Stationary, inert, waiting for something good to happen soon) thats why I have enclosed letter to Fiona Pitt-Kethley what a mouthful as she would say. Hope Mrs Mary Shitehouse was not watching last night. Anyway must stop now 2am watching Boxing Match always awake and always watching night TV on TVS from 11pm to 5/6 AM. Hope you will reply to me, and pass on my letter to Fiona Pitt-Kethley.

Your everawake Knight Sir Francis Drake.

A selection of poems written to, or about, me:

The following poem was written after its author read in the *Daily Mail* that I had attended a Betjeman Society do:

Miss F. Pitt Keighley meets Sir John's Ghost at the Betjeman Memorial Function

Miss Fiona Pitt keighley
I do declare
I was, though a ghost,
Rather surprised, to read
You were there.

In my lifetime
i hope that i tried

to keep poetrys muse
an elegant bride.

I sought not to deface her
And to lift up the heart
Why miss pitt keighley debase her
and then call it art?

Old gents in raincoats
making advances
were not my material
nor were lewd glances.

perhaps in the fashion
of feminine rule
you aspire to the laureates crown
or am I being cruel
re your journey to town?

Now miss j. hunter dunne
was rather good fun
and your'e double barrelled too
but i must end
Ive a penny to spend
Even ghosts have to go to the loo!

*   *   *

FEELING CLOSE (below) was written by headless Mike,
mentioned in *The Book Trade*.

Oh the joy, the absolute joy of being together,
Caressing each other as only strangers can do,
Indeed neither weighing thoughts nor measuring words
But secure in the knowledge that life should be enjoyed to
the full.

*   *   *

You kindled in my heart, a secret little flame,
That refuses to go out, and longs to play the game.
This feeling that I have, I know will last forever,
Or until I get the chance, to touch you in the heather.

by another Michael.

The following poem is the P.S. to another and records the
temporary confiscation of a copy of *Journeys to the Under-
world* at Kennedy Airport.

Last Thursday, your *Journeys* was snatched in the Shed,
Of all places, at Kennedy, as I sought but a bed.
Not porno, I assured the man at the Gate,
Oh, give me the book, I'm tired and it's late.

'But it's signed by the dame, a looker as well,
Do you know this piece, Mac, she looks pretty swell?'
A casual flick, and oh – just my luck,
It is Ostia – and Roberto, the standing buck.

The book it came back, after ages and ages,
The cover well thumbed, as were the pages.
'But Mac, on your way to find you that bed,
Next time, through that Channel, the one that is Red!'

P.W.

Reply by *The Perfect Man* to the title poem of my last
collection:

THE PERFECT WOMAN

AMSTRAD to AMSTRAD
For such was her preferred mode
As violet ink caused SUCH OFFENSE.

Black-haired, enviably-muscled
She sat down for tea – the perfect host.
He had not expected her mother's conversation to be
livelier than hers
So anxiously he racked his 'slow academic brains'
To stir the dying conversation
Uncomfortably talking about
Portentous this (LITERATURE)
Not to mention that (OPERA)
Certainly not quizzing the Perfect Woman for Marriage.

She offered him (kindly as it seemed)
Four volumes of Scott – then a favourite author
Gladly but naively accepted as a gift
Not realising that they merely made a space
For authors much more treasured
Ian Fleming – or perhaps Sheridan Le Fanu.

Her final letter was something of a shock
The Other Man was waiting for her chez Valerie
Hence, and not because of a non-screwing Scot,
The silence.

Even though Ovid's godesses 'love to fuck'
Was there screwing in Horace or Virgil? –
Sources (she said) for her Travel Book
She did say it was an easy word to find a rhyme for
Her book more sucking than looking, she might have said.

But then, the greatest shocks of all:
Page 39
Not to mention – nay, an A Level question c. 2001
Compare and contrast: pages 73, and, pages 79–80.

I don't quite understand all *The Perfect Man*'s allusions to
page numbers, non-screwing Scots, etc. and I have never had
black hair – well, only for a week or so and long before I met
him. He is wrong in his assumptions about Horace and Virgil,
of course. What on earth did he think Dido and Aeneas got up

to in that cave? He should also read Horace's satires. He is right however about me preferring Ian Fleming and Sheridan le Fanu to Scott.

The following offering came with a bottle of bath oil by Floris St James.

A little present I bought in Town,
please accept without a frown.
A little something for being kind
for checking how my verses rhymed

I'll dream of you in soft warm water
although Fiona I did'nt oughter
And in my dream I'll gently swim
through fragrant waters to your quim.

Oh what a thrill to make it there
and nuzzle in your pubic hair.
Then gliding o'er your mound of venus
your soft moist lips anoint my penis.

Then up and up till my balls rest
in union with your perfect nest
Encircling arms then hold me tight
and we stay together through the night.

by a retired squadron leader.

I replied with a one-line postcard, quoting Graves: 'Down, wanton down!'